YOUTUBE GROWTH SECRETS I THE YOUTUBE FORMULA I COMPLETE SEO GUIDE I JOURNEY OF SUCCESSFUL YOUTUBER

HOW TO BE SUCCESSFUL YOUTUBER AND EARN MONEY

CHANDRA MOHAN SAH

This book is dedicated to my friends who told me that having information and telling it to someone is a different thing and I will not be able to do it. This negative talk has inspired me so that I can write such a useful book.

Also I would like to thank my wife who kept encouraging me.

Contents

Preface

CHANDRA MOHAN SAH helps others to expand the leverage technology to their reach (and revenue) with reduced stress and no drama. He does this with a lifestyle and business designed to answer the challenges and opportunities of today's ever changing information economy. If you are looking for titles, he is a husband, father, author, podcaster, and CEO of **mymlmleader.com**, **merahindiblog.com** and **walletbudy.com**. He lives in India.

The Education Background of author is very rich. Author having honors degree in Political Science from University of Delhi, Master Degree in Public Administration from Himachal Pradesh University, Shimla, Law Degree from University of Delhi. Along with this author is having technical knowledge of Computer/software too.

Author is also blogger, YouTuber, affiliate marketer and network marketer having more than 18 year experience.

So without going any deeper let's start...........

Prologue

About This Book

This is not a Book about the Tech of YouTube!

My goal is to teach you that with YouTube, a "Ready, Aim, Fire" approach is the best. I've seen too many people "Fire" first... and the results are never good.

This is a book of YouTube SEO Complete Guide - how to think about YouTube, how to understand what you are getting yourself into, and how to use the strategies to "start right." Understand what you are doing first, before you take on the tech.

This is not a Book of Only my Content and Ideas

I have a number of bonus chapters in this book that bring a well-rounded examination of all things YouTube. The authors are the best of the best, and it's an honor to have them in this book.

CHAPTER ONE

Ideal Length for a YouTube Video?

People ask this every time: what is the ideal video length for YouTube? And most common answer is "nobody watches video more than three minutes and people like to watch shorts video." People make these blanket statements of absolute nonsense, so let's take the time to walk through these myths.

Reality: the concept that people only watch short videos online is not true. If you think about it logically, YouTube has spent millions of dollars putting up full-length concerts, all-day festivals and other all-day events simply because people do consume long-form content.

People are making full length vlog, now vlog is latest trend on YouTube platform. YouTube would not spend millions putting up long-form content if people didn't watch it.

The reason why most videos are only three minutes or shorts in length is because most people only have three minutes of content to say. Or, they are building YouTube Shorts videos for an audience with short video attention spans.

If you only have three minutes of content or short video to say, and you have an audience with a three-minute attention span, obviously deal with that audience; but the idea that only short videos are consumed is absolutely ridiculous.

If you want to leave the world of YouTube, consider Hulu, which has hour-long television shows, or Netflix, with feature length films. People are willing (and happy) to consume full-length content online if it is good.

So what is the ideal video length?

How long should you make your video? <u>**The answer is actually quite simple: make your video as long as it needs to be and not one minute**</u>

<u>longer.</u>

The fact of the matter is, you have to know your audience to make that decision. You have to know what it is they are looking for and you have to deliver the right content for them. Understand that they can click out – they can go anywhere they want – and that there are a myriad of competitors for the very piece of information you are trying to stream on YouTube. <u>For that reason, the video needs to be as long as it needs to be; and not one minute – actually, not one second – longer.</u>

So what are the action items? What can you do?

In this present ear we have massive hard drives, unlimited upload space and the ability to send hours of video to YouTube.

Make your video part of the content; but again, do that quickly. Another tip for you is to tell your viewer how long your video is up front; it helps tremendously. What would you rather watch, a video called "Social Media Marketing" or a video called "Social Media Marketing Explained in 3 Minutes and 7 Seconds?" Think about it; I've got three minutes so I'll give that a go. So it can be a strategic implementation, but don't worry about going longer if you need to. Serve your audience; don't worry about a magic number.

CHAPTER TWO

What Equipment and Software Required to Create a Good Quality Video?

If you are going to be YouTuber or Blogger or Podcaster then some basic Equipment and Software is required for good quality video and Audio. If you have sufficient money then you must purchase a high definition camera.

A High Definition Camera can be purchased fewer than 20k to 30k. You may explore through given link.

First, you need a high-definition (HD) camera. But high definition camera on your phone is probably good enough for what you need to do. If HD camera on your phone is good, you can get even better ones, if required by your work.

Secondly, more important than the video is the audio quality. I've seen some YouTuber who have Rs. 20,000/- to Rs. 35,000/- phone cameras, but 35,000/ or Rs. 50,000/- audio rigs, because the audio is actually more important than the camera image.

We need high-definition camera? Yes, because you want to upload in high-definition quality to YouTube so that the viewer takes you seriously. Audio is still more important. There are several great microphones for under Rs. 1000/- to 5,000/- you can do your homework by visiting a site like Amazon and looking for the most highly-ranked equipment. **My favorite options are listed in the "Chandra Mohan Sah's Favorite Tech" chapter of this book.**

Thirdly, next most important requirement is the lighting. If you can afford it, examine three-point lighting, which you can search for in your favorite search engine (YouTube has video after video that explains how to utilize this method).

One alternative, if you don't have good lighting equipment, then go outside to Mother Nature where there is good organic lighting (though obviously, don't go out shooting in the middle of a storm). However, know that lighting is the also most important aspect of your video production behind audio.

A good **quality video option can also be a screen cast video**, which is a video recording of your screen. The video that I initially created for this book was a screen cast video that's been extremely profitable for me. With screen casting, you don't need good lighting and camera.

You are just required a screen casting software or app and mic for your mobile and computer. I have provide quality name and link of software and mobile application in the end of this book for your help.

Finally, in terms of traditional video editing, iMovie on the Mac works well. Whatever version of iMovie you have is great, and you can download it from the Apple store. Video editing is also playing great roll for your video. If you don't edit your video as per content or requirement then you will never get success on YouTube platform or any other video creator platform.

So, my recommendation is KineMaster Which is free with this book. A downloading link is also available in the end of this book. Beside this software you can also use another video editing software which available for your smartphone/mac/laptop, I am talking about Filmora, Inshot which can be used without any watermark. You may also take membership as per your requirement. Above software can be used with laptop and mobile too.

CHAPTER THREE

How to use YouTube Annotations & End Screen?

Have you noticed something while playing YouTube Video? Like pop-ups, Text, Links in different colors, these all are part of YouTube system/ platform. Do you know, YouTube is working diligently, spending millions of dollars to integrate this across all of the platforms, including television and mobile? So you can understand that YouTube Annotation is very important for your videos. I can understand that what you are thinking?

What do you do with that? How do you use them? How do you make them part of your business?

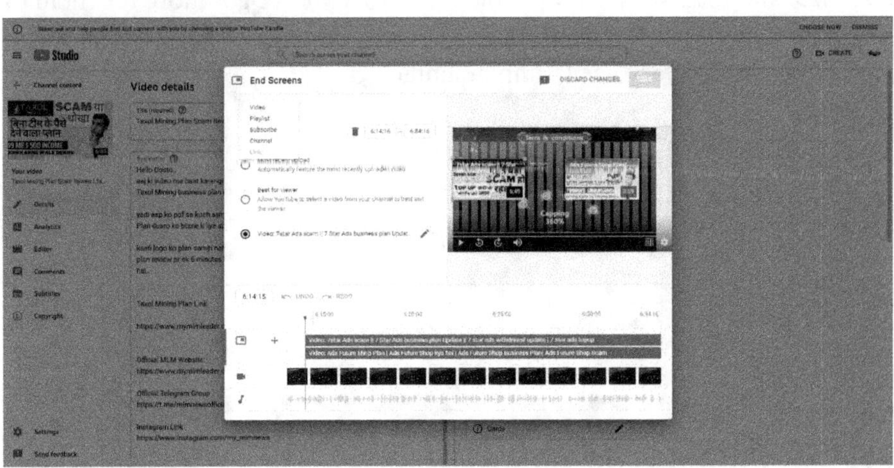

Annotations & End Screen?

Annotations/end screen bring integration, they bring interactivity, and they bring some very cool things into the online video process.

One thing you can do with link – and that's a powerful facet of Annotations/end screen. At the time of uploading the video, you are able to link to other YouTube videos. Just think that somebody has just found your Channel or video and they're watching a video that they like; when they reach the end of the video and they want more, you should certainly tell them, **"I have more, here's a video about X".** The great thing about Annotations/end screen is that when viewers click on one, it takes them directly to that video. So you can insert link of your YouTube video for getting more view and watch time.

You can also link to a playlist, simply by saying, "If you like this type of video, I've made more videos on this topic," and provide a link to that list. You should realize as well that the playlist can come up in YouTube results, so you have effectively double power there.

In the end of this, there is an option to include annotation links to merchandise providers. YouTube has a list of ones that you can use, so do check the list. You may also link your blog or website so you can earn extra money by adsense ads.

What are the action items? What can you do with all these choices?

Please make sure that use of annotations should be in sense. For example, including a subscribe annotation in every single videos makes complete and total sense. Let people know that you've got more for them to see by linking to playlists and linking to other videos; all of these ideas are very strategic and very easily implemented.

CHAPTER FOUR

Use of YouTube Cards.

YouTube annotations and Cards are 90% similar. But as per my experience and updates from YouTube, YouTube Cards may replace annotations in future. YouTube describes Cards as the evolution of Annotations. Right now you can use both the tools for your videos.

YouTube Cards and Annotations are very useful if you want to encourage your viewers to take an action, like Subscribe, go to another video or associated website, etc.

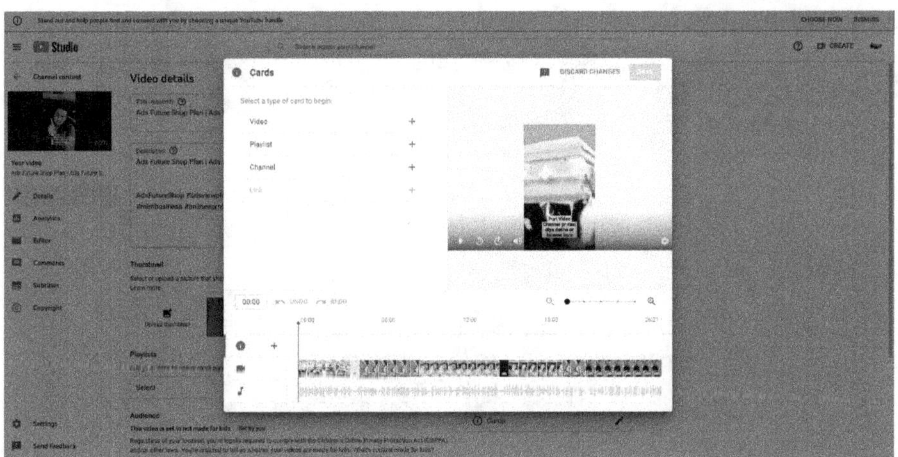

Cards

Differences between cards and annotations

The main difference between annotation and cards is their outlook. Cards are more graphical whereas annotations are text based. The cards slide in once you click the small "i" button on the video where as the annotation is there based on the timings set by the user.

1. YouTube Cards are small and unobtrusive, unless a viewer chooses to click on them, which is why they are the better option when you are trying to get views on other videos. Irritating a few people with a big annotation might be worth it if you also draw other people's attention to your cause or website, but it is not a good way to endear yourself to people you are trying to get views and subscriptions from.When a card is clicked a thumbnail will appear with a link to your additional content. YouTube Cards are often better than annotations for adding links to your videos because they look much tidier. Also, unlike annotations, cards will be visible to people watching your videos on their mobile devices.

2. You cannot use Cards just to insert notes into your videos, though, and you cannot adjust their size like you can with annotations. So, if you do need a link to be large and extremely noticeable, annotations might still be your best option. Cards and annotations can even be used in combination sometimes.

CHAPTER FIVE

How to Shoot Videos

Shooting a videos are art, some creators just shoot the video without any planning or work and upload the same on YouTube platform. Due to this they do not get any result. If you want real result or money with your videos and want to be a successful YouTuber then you have to follow certain guidance as under:-

Step1. Define the goal of your video.

First, you think, what is goal of your video? Do you want to promote your brand or want to share some information? Here I am very much clear that your one goal is income, Yes ! you want to make money with your videos.

In view of above, before recording your video keep in your mind that requirement of people/viewer. What are they looking for? So give them what they want and shorten their learning curve.

Step 2. Create a script or outline for your videos.

Get your ideas down on paper. Depending on your comfort level in front of the camera you may want to use a teleprompter (like I do) or at the very least bullet points to keep the flow of your video moving. Just make sure that if you are using a teleprompter that your voice doesn't sound like you are reading. Keep your energy level up and sound enthusiastic. I use a phrase with my clients called "Talking past the lens" which means projecting your voice past the camera. I like to visualize the viewer watching you at home in this tiny little video window on their computer. It's a small window, so you've got to project and be interesting or else the viewer will click away. Don't be afraid of that scary lens; make the camera your new best friend.

Step 3. Create a visual Bible.

What do I mean by that? A visual Bible is simply a list of visual ideas and concepts that you want to incorporate in your videos. What do you want your video to look like? What's the look of your set or background going to be?

What is the feel and tone of your video? How do you want the audience to feel when they see your video? What kind of music will help convey this feeling? Keep working towards these ideas until you achieve them.

<u>Step 4. Try to build connection with your audience.</u>

In the end of video, you may share your struggle story with your audience. Try to tell about you topic and your niche.

<u>Step 5. Review your video before publishing on YouTube platform</u>

After shooting your video, always review the video and see, is there any need to add or remove content. If You see that something missing then reshoot the video with cool mind.

<u>Step 6. Promotion of your Videos</u>

There are some famous Social Platform like Facebook, Twitter, Instagram, pinterest etc. You should make a profile of your channel and share your every video on such platform.

I hope these tips would be helpful to you.

CHAPTER SIX

Camera Required or Not for Your Video?

First of all I would say that **camera is required for shooting** YouTube Videos. But there are some categories in which you may create decent video. If you don't want a camera these categories will help you. I am giving all the details

1. **Screencast Video**

Screencasting is a very good optin for YouTube videos. You can record your computer screen using a program called "Screenflow" for the Mac (look it up in App Store) and "Camtasia" for Windows machines.

If You want to make a video with the help of your smartphone then there so many app available for Android and iOS. You may download your own.

1. **Animation Video**

If you use Google Search or YouTube then you will find so many tools that will create animation video from pre designed template. You may customize according to your story or niche. You may use it free or paid.

3. **Outsourcing of Videos**

If you don't want to purchase HD Camera or don't want to shoot video then you can outsource video for your channel. You may find so many creator at Fiverr, upwork etc.

CHAPTER SEVEN

Use of Music- Prevent Copyright

Music is the very important part of any videos. You should use music sound according to your video. But there are some points to remember:-

1. Always use rights full video for your YouTube or obtain a license from the music provider. 2nd option is that always use royalty free music. If you don't do this you may receive a copyright issue and this is not good for your channel.

1. Please use soft music and it should not too loud to cover narration/ your voice. Sometimes constant music works, but more times than not, silence is a great emphasis that punctuates the entrance of a new theme.

3. If you see copyrighted music on YouTube, don't think it's legal and you can also use that music. If you are using any copyrighted music for your personal use, you will not receive any copyright. But if you are going to use that music for your commercial use then copyright is there.

4. Always use music from YouTube Music Library to avoid copyright or give credit to original creator.

CHAPTER EIGHT

What to do after publishing Video?

You made the video and published the same, now what is the next step to follow to gain subscriber and view?

Some of the YouTubers try to buy view which is not good for channel, you may lose your channel and defiantly you don't want it.

You can do two thing after publishing your YouTube Video.

1. When you publish a video after that send it to all the social media channels or platform and your social group. Once Google See this, Google will react accordingly.
2. If you have a list of people/email then sends your video to them. It's good for marketing or selling any products.

CHAPTER NINE

How to Rank YouTube Video on the front of Google or YouTube?

This is the most important questions for any new your old YouTuber. After shooting video you can publish your video but how to get more view or rank on that video? Here, I am going to tell you some tips. I will also share my personal experience.

Before shooting any video you should know the facts about Google is in the business of delivering best result for user. If you don't deliver best result then people will leave you soon. So help Google to do their job and Google/YouTube will help your video get seen.

"If you do a search on anything and see nine text results and one video option, where are you most likely to click? If you are looking for information, what would you rather do: read or watch? Search engines are a medium of instant gratification and video does a much better job of that. You know this; Google knows this; now it is time to act on what we know."

Now you can understand that Google want to deliver good result to users, so make the best video for Google Search Result.

What should you do?

1. The title for your video should include the keyword that people are looking for.
2. Use Keyword in the first sentence of the description of the video.
3. Use tags according to video and title.
4. Make Playlist of Video.
5. Use atleast 500 words in video description. It's good for SEO.

6. Make your video according to taste of viewers.
7. Keyword Research
8. Share your video link to community tab.

These are the small task to do but they play very important role behind the video. So, never forget to include these things.

CHAPTER TEN

Is it better to have one YouTube Channel for Everything I do or different as per niche?

This is a very important question and it's a great strategy question that absolutely makes sense.

Starting smart is always better than fixing things later.

Is it better to have one YouTube channel for everything or a separate YouTube channel for every niche you happen to find yourself involved with? **<u>MY ANSWER WOULD BE NO</u>**

If you are going to start a YouTube Channel then you must know that there are different people with different choices.

As you know that YouTube accounts are free and you can sign up for a different account or channel, because they are free and because the option is always there. Use this feature and create another channel for another topic of niche. For Example : If I like to watch some business review then I will search business related video or channel, if you upload different type of videos in one channel then it will make messy, people cannot understand what type channel is it. If they get confuse then they will leave your channel.

Always create channel according niche and upload video accordingly. If you are making video for children then upload content for children only.

<u>Moreover, there are actually a few benefits of having multiple channels.</u>

Remember that you can cross-promote channels. If you have numbers of channels, each of the channels can promote back to one channel, and you can create a network. There are certainly some internal ranking features that exist there and it's good for SEO.

Is it better to have one channel for everything or one per niche? I would say one per niche, unless that's going to be a distraction for you... and that's something only you can answer.

CHAPTER ELEVEN

When Should I Let YouTube place Ads on Videos?

As per latest Rules of YouTube Ads Partnership, minimum 1000 subscribers and total 4000 hours watch hours are required to monetize YouTube Channel/Videos in one year. If you reached this requirement then you channel would be monetized by YouTube. After that you or your viewers can see ads on your video and you will start earning money from those ads.

Letting YouTube place ads on your videos just for the cash doesn't make sense unless you go viral or you're just the type of person who has millions of people viewing your videos. If you can pull that off, great. But in reality, ads are just a lot more work and a lot more effort than many people make it out to be.

If you want to earn from YouTube Ads then make trendy, informative video for people. Again, you should realize that YouTube makes money from the ads. As a result, YouTube looks at all the partners and says, "Which of the partners have I made money from? Which of the channels have I made money from?" Those are the ones that they are going to promote the most. So if you include ads on a couple of videos, you are going to do better on your YouTube channel than people who don't.

<u>Monetization of YouTube Shorts/Shorts Funds</u>

In the beginning of 2023, YouTubers or creators in the YouTube Partner Program will be eligible to monetize their Shorts videos. Now creators will earn money from ads that run between videos in the Shorts Feeds.

YouTube will add the revenue generated from ads in the Shorts feed and pay out a share to creators at the end of the month. From the overall amount allocated to creators, they will keep 45% of the revenue, distributed based on their share of total Shorts views.

<u>Expanding YouTube Partner Program Eligibility</u>

To benefit from Shorts monetization, creators must first get accepted into the YouTube Partner Program.

To get more Shorts-focused creators into the Partner Program, YouTube is introducing new eligibility criteria.

Starting in early 2023, creators can apply to the YouTube Partner Program by meeting a threshold of 1,000 subscribers and 10M Shorts views over 90 days.

This change will allow creators to qualify for the Partner Program even if they don't publish long-form videos.

When this change rolls out, YouTube will keep its existing criteria in place — which is 1,000 subscribers and 4,000 watch hours.

Lastly, YouTube says it will lower the qualifying threshold for fan funding in early 2023, allowing non-Partner Program creators to make money from viewer purchases.

In addition to Shorts-specific funding, YouTube's also lowering its thresholds to qualify for monetization via YPP, which will give more people access to fan funding elements, including Super Thanks and Super Stickers (including Shorts creators), while it's also developing new funding avenues for live-streamers as well.

CHAPTER TWELVE

Some Important Points to remember while shooting Your Videos?

1. Topic

If you are thinking of making a YouTube channel or video, then first of all you should know that on which topic you want to create a YouTube Channel. To Create YouTube Channel, you must have a good topic/niche so that you can make a video on that topic/nice.

If you have made a channel without thinking, it is only a waste of time and your hard work. Therefore, before making a channel, clear the topic in your mind, and then only go ahead.

Produce the best quality video you can both in format and content and take the time required to upload it to YouTube, even if your audience can't consume it today.

2. Knowledge

After the topic, the second most important thing comes that of knowledge. Choosing an easy topic is more difficult than that, if you do not have the knowledge of that topic, then you cannot post more than just 2-4 videos. Therefore, you should take only that topic which you have good knowledge of. With knowledge, you can keep posting new videos, from which your channel will go far and you will start earning money too.

3. Smartphone

To make videos for YouTube, it is enough for you to have a basic Smartphone. You do not need to get a separate camera. When your channel goes a little, then you can take a camera according to your budget. Many new YouTubers take expensive gadgets in the beginning and they do not even know properly on which topic to make videos.

4. Video Quality

Whenever you shoot a video, keep in mind that you shoot in HD, nowadays even a basic smartphone has the facility to shoot HD video. You will benefit from HD Video that YouTube will promote your video because HD Video YouTube promotes more and more quickly.

5. Video Title

Keep the title of your video in such a way that it matches with your video and is the latest one which is also going viral on YouTube. Only then people will click on your video and watch your video, you can take the help of Keyword Planner for the title of your video.

6. Attractive Thumbnail

The thumbnail of your video is more important than the title of the video because the viewer first of all sees your thumbnail and clicks on your video. The thumbnail should be very clean and as per your video.

CHAPTER THIRTEEN

What can you do more with YouTube?

YouTube has made some changes in the last year that have, quite honestly, surprised. It's always fun to guess as to what's coming next on any platform. In many ways, we have no more idea of what's coming to YouTube.

Social Integration

Social integration is the future of the internet. All types of content will be tightly integrated into social networking: media, text, search, commerce etc. If you think about it, it makes total sense that social integration is so powerful.

360 Degree Videos

Do you know that YouTube supports a 360 degree video format that lets you view the video from any angle? It's now not a perfect technology and is currently only supported on the browser. The audience embracing this new technology doesn't seem to have passed the fascination stage at this point.

Integrated Commerce

YouTube has some integrated commerce capabilities. You can link from your YouTube video to iTunes and Amazon, or even to your own store at the popular ecommerce platform Shopify.

CHAPTER FOURTEEN

My Favorite Tech
<u>Hardware</u>

1. Canon M50 Mark

    Buy from here :- https://amzn.to/3VC0XiZ
    Features

- In-camera YouTube live streaming for real-time video engagement
- Film vertical videos in 4K for social media; Wireless connectivity with smartphone and cloud storage
- Vertical Vlogging Made Easy; Stay Steady and in Control
- Record in Stunning 4K Resolution; Stay in Focus All the Time; Ready, Touch, Action!
- Photo Sensor Technology: Cmos; Compatible Mountings: Canon Ef-M; Hardware Interface: 802 11 Bgn; Wireless Communication Technology: Wi-Fi

1. Canon EOS 1500D 24.1 Digital SLR Camera

    Buy form here :- https://amzn.to/3MJV1Al

- Sensor: APS-C CMOS Sensor with 24.1 MP (high resolution for large prints and image cropping). Transmission frequency (central frequency):Frequency: 2 412 to 2 462MHz. Standard diopter :-2.5 - +0.5m-1 (dpt)
- ISO: 100-6400 sensitivity range (critical for obtaining grain-free pictures, especially in low light)
- Image Processor: DIGIC 4+ with 9 autofocus points (important for speed and accuracy of autofocus and burst photography)

- Video Resolution: Full HD video with fully manual control and selectable frame rates (great for precision and high-quality video work)
- Connectivity: WiFi, NFC and Bluetooth built-in (useful for remotely controlling your camera and transferring pictures wirelessly as you shoot)
- Lens Mount: EF-S mount compatible with all EF and EF-S lenses (crop-sensor mount versatile and compact, especially when used with EF-S lenses)

Microphone

3. Metronaut Wireless Lavalier Microphone Mic System

    Buy from here :- https://amzn.to/3s7qZgt
    Best for YouTube, Facebook Live Stream TikTok Video Recording Vlog for Type-C Android & iPhone, Plug and Play, No Need APP & Bluetooth

4. Amazpro (CONETNT CREATOR CHOICE :15 YEARS WARRANTY) Plug-Play Wireless Lavalier Microphone

    Buy from here :- https://amzn.to/3gnlGa0

Best for Video Recording, YouTube Facebook Live Stream, Vlog, Wireless Mic for USB-C Andriod Phones, Tablet and Computer(No Need App/Bluetooth)

Software

1. Camtasia (Screen Recorder) 2. Canva (For everything) 3. Filmora 4. Kinemaster

    Download KineMaster from here:- https://drive.google.com/file/d/1asjYxgfRs_2ZmKGAENrMw-C2LrrRvGPI/view?usp=drivesdk